GOING THROUGH
2 BECOME

GOING THROUGH 2 BECOME

VANESSA WILLIAMS LOYD

XULON PRESS

Xulon Press
2301 Lucien Way #415
Maitland, FL 32751
407.339.4217
www.xulonpress.com

Unless otherwise indicated, Scripture quotations taken from the King James Version (KJV)–*public domain.*

Scripture quotations taken from the New King James Version (NKJV). Copyright © 1982 by Thomas Nelson, Inc. Used by permission. All rights reserved.

Scripture quotations taken from the English Standard Version (ESV). Copyright © 2001 by Crossway, a publishing ministry of Good News Publishers. Used by permission. All rights reserved.

Scripture quotations taken from the Holy Bible, New International Version (NIV). Copyright © 1973, 1978, 1984, 2011 by Biblica, Inc.™. Used by permission. All rights reserved.

Scripture quotations taken from The Living Bible (TLB). Copyright © 1971 by Tyndale House Foundation. Used by permission of Tyndale House Publishers Inc., Carol Stream, Illinois 60188. All rights reserved.

Printed in the United States of America.

ISBN-13: 978-1-6322-1860-5
Ebook: 978-1-6322-1861-2

DEDICATION

This book is dedicated to my Mother, who has been my inspiration and such a tremendous example of Love and Faithfulness to God. Through all of her trials she never gave up on The Lord, but modeled what it means to be a true Woman of God. I'm grateful she doesn't have to suffer any longer and I look forward to seeing her one day in glory!

GRATITUDE

I thank God for the opportunity to write this book. I thank all of you who have supported me, prayed for me, and watched over me as I've struggled to live the precepts of this book. I am thankful to my husband Michael, who supports this work, to my children who are my biggest cheerleaders, always ready with a "you can do it Mommy", and to my Church Family who is ready and willing to aide me in any way they can. Thanks to all of you for your support.

This book is written for all types of people. There are so many things in this nation and world that divide us. We are known by people groups, geography, social status, race, religion, and more. But there is a simple topic uniting us, which is relatable to all because, as the Bible tells us, "Man who is born of woman is of few days and full of trouble" (Job 14:1 NKJ). One thing for sure is this: If we live long enough, we are all going to go through something!

About the Bible verses in this book:

Each time a Bible verse is quoted, I provide the translation it came from, noted by the following abbreviations:

- KJV: King James Bible
- NKJ: New King James Version
- ESV: English Standard Version
- NIV: New International Version
- TLB: The Living Bible

CONTENTS

FOREWORD

Perspective is something we all have need of when it comes to our relationship with God and the life we experience. At times it may even seem paradoxical. The Scriptures are full of stories of people who sought God and found Him, but only through great trials. We can gain perspective through various experiences in our own lives which serve to deepen our understanding and provide solutions to problems; but this may also leave us feeling unsettled in our walk with God. However, when we look outside ourselves, we can see the lives of others, and their experiences can shine light on our own situations.

A new perspective can be gained through education, reading, work experiences, marriage, being a parent, and watching your children become parents. In this book, author Vanessa Loyd (my mother) invites you to share in the perspective from all of those examples and more from her own experiences. She has gleaned several truths that are relevant and necessary in order to understand God on a deeper level and to understand our own experiences properly.

I have been blessed throughout my life to learn these truths and more, not only from her words, but also in the way she lived her life. I am thrilled beyond words she accepted the calling to share them with you. I pray (but also know) this book will provide you with perspective and insight about your own personal experiences; and serve to help you hold fast to your faith in these last days. May God's blessings and His Spirit ever guide you as you learn more about Him, and may the words of this book speak to and strengthen your soul.

Justin Loyd,
Author
"Simple Plans" and "Custom Christians"

PURPOSE

*T*he purpose of this book is to expose and clarify erroneous beliefs surrounding the idea of "Going Through."

1. If you are "going through" then you must have done something wrong to deserve it.

2. To show proof that if something bad happens, it doesn't mean it is a result of committing some sin; and therefore being punished.

3. To have an honest dialog as to why it is imperative we tell the truth when people give their lives to Christ. We must set true expectations. **You are not on easy street!**

4. Just because your testimony doesn't end in God coming through in the nick of time, doesn't mean you're not in the Plan and Will of God. More likely, it didn't turn out like you wanted or expected.

INTRODUCTION

I am writing this book because I believe it is a personal mandate to me from God to share with people on going through hard times. I don't pretend to know why He chose me to do this. I just know that if I don't do it I would feel as if I had completely and deliberately disobeyed God. Let me say up front, that is not an area I frequent! I am sad and broken when I miss God and do the wrong thing, getting caught up in the flesh and disobeying Him. Honestly, I wish He hadn't chosen me for this task. It has meant I have had to "go through" and am still "going through" many things personally to get this book written. However, with that said, I'm not going to disobey on purpose. With that disclaimer, let me begin.

I must confess that I've not always known the ways and things of God, or even walked with God, as I try to do at this point in my life. Even though my father was a preacher and my mom loved God with all her heart and soul. The church we grew up in didn't teach a lot about a relationship with Christ, so I didn't get to "know" God until I was in my mid-twenties. I am number thirteen out of fifteen children, the wife of a minister, a minister myself, mother of three children, and raised, two special needs nephews. I have survived financial devastation, the death of three siblings, plus my mother and father, empty nest syndrome, menopause, and many more challenges life has thrown my way. Some seasons have seemed to last forever. I felt like I just wasn't going to make it. On top of all of that, plenty of good ole' church folk told me along the way that I must have done something wrong to deserve all the challenges I've faced.

I've suffered multiple broken bones over the years, starting with my sister dropping me down the stairs when I was a baby. That resulted in one leg being shorter than the other for a while. I've almost drowned at least twice. I've been in several car accidents where the cars were totaled and it was declared I should have been dead. I have been raped. I have been in a robbery at gun point. This list could go on of the challenges I've lived through. Through it all of it I believe God has kept me alive for a reason. Even for such a time as this. It wasn't luck or chance that I'm still here. No one in my family ever thought I would live to be twenty-five years old. I was so accident prone and always getting sick. I almost bled to death because of a tooth extraction. Given these events, I believe I have some experience which allows me to discuss what "Going Through To Become" really means.

One of my goals in this book is to encourage all of you who have ever gone through tough times (or will go through them) to be confident that God is still with you no matter what the situation is! You may be going through right now. If not, live long enough and you will (as my momma used to say). If I can share something that gives you the confidence that it is perfectly okay, totally natural, and definitely in God's plan for us all to "go through"; then I will have accomplished what I believe God would have me do in this book.

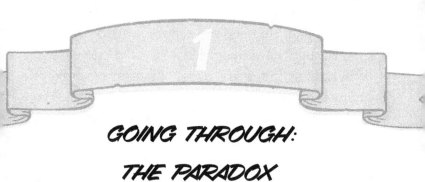

GOING THROUGH:
THE PARADOX

*H*elp! There's a war going on and it's in my body! The things I want to do I find myself not doing. I know what's right, what I should do, but somehow I find myself doing just the opposite. This is the paradoxical situation we find ourselves faced with each and every day. We throw up our hands and say, "What next? I can't take it anymore, why do I have to go through this? It's always something!" Why doesn't God just make us do what He wants us to do? He already knew this flesh was going to be a mess. It wants to do only what it wants to do, and when it wants to do it! Who wants to do good "all" the time anyway? There's no fun in that!

In this book I will explore this paradox and other concepts about what "going through" really means, and how it affects every aspect of our lives.

The number-one truth about "going through" is that, in all reality and in most instances, we really don't have a clue why we are going through it. With that in mind, we need to examine why some of our first thoughts are things like, what did I do wrong? Why has this happened to me? What area of sin exists in my life that God won't or hasn't blessed me? We see other people being blessed and we say, "Why not me, Lord? When is my turn coming?" And somehow we all manage to hear some version of this phrase from our number-one arch enemy, Satan. **"It's because you missed it, you did something wrong!"** And when we listen to that voice we are deceived! It adds to our devastation. It makes us wonder what we could have done to cause this situation. We question whether it's our fault, if we deserve to be punished and ultimately, if God is so loving, why has He allowed this to happen?

When we think of "going through", we think of difficulties we have to face. In our lives there will be many challenges to experience. Sometimes it will be something that is happening on a regular basis. Another time

> *"It's because you missed it, you did sometwhing wrong"*

it may be a one-time thing. Or it may be a series of events that occur one right after another. These difficulties may come in the form of trials, persecutions, tribulations or afflictions.

Whenever these difficulties arise, we can't help but recognize they are situations we must deal with whether we want to or not. They *demand* some type of response from us. Our flesh screams for us to do something! In some situations, we can take some course of action that might change it, but at other times there is nothing we can do. Yet our emotions hold us hostage,

> *This proclivity in our flesh toward sin causes us to war against our own spiritual inside!*

because we desire an immediate escape from the torturous challenge we are going through. We feel as if we can't take the things that are happening or have already happened that are causing us pain and angst. We hear a voice inside our heads saying, "Do something, do something."

When we cannot remedy the circumstance, we are weighed down and discontented with our lives! Feelings of hopelessness arise and we feel condemned because we have no control over what is happening. Does that sound like anything you've ever felt? Has that ever happened in your life and you've literally despaired of relief? Well, welcome to the club! It is a part of this thing called *life*. Situations will come up that leave your head spinning. You wonder how in the world did this situation happen?

And even bigger still is the question of how will you get yourself out?

There are things we want to do in life and we know that we should do. Some things we even feel God has told us to do, but somehow we find ourselves doing just the opposite. We forget we are people of destiny and purpose. The Bible says, "And we know all things work together for good to them that love God, to them who are the called according to *His* purpose" (Romans 8:28 NKJ). We also see in the book of Psalms, "I cry out to God Most High, to God who fulfills His purpose for me" (Psalm 57:2 ESV).

The nature of the paradox is that inside of us on the one hand is the innate desire to be and do what God has purposed us to be. But on the other hand also inside us is the desire of our flesh which is shaped in iniquity and conceived in sin according to Psalm 51:5. **This proclivity in our flesh toward sin causes us to war against our own spiritual inside!** It wants to do something totally different, so we find ourselves in a place where we have to go through certain things to become what God wants us to be, what God wants us to represent on a daily basis in our lives. The process to overcome this paradox is part of the renewing of our minds and the transformation of our lives into what we were predestined for and purposed to do.

2

GOING THROUGH: WHAT IT IS AND HOW WE RESPOND

Situations we see as "going through" are numerous and varied. Some examples we may have to go through include marital challenges, injustices we face, child-related issues, economic setbacks, unexpected extended illness, death of loved ones, and any kind of relationship challenges in our work, church or home.

"Going through" is the process that takes place as we deal with difficult situations that arise in our lives! It means being put in or exposed to a position of difficulty, stress, challenge, or tragedy. During these times we may feel pressured, anxious, upset, unhappy,

> *"Going through" is the process that takes place as we deal with difficult situations that arise in our lives.*

depressed, disappointed, confused, out of sorts, and much more.

"Going through" is a major challenge to our flesh. The bottom line is this: **any time we don't get what we want, when we want it, we feel we are "going through"**! Therefore, I've found it to be a very subjective thing. What it means to me and what it means to you may be very different. Certainly the things you are "going through" might be things I may not feel are really "going through" and vice versa. You may look upon the things I call "going through" and feel they are not at all difficult. But one thing for sure we all have in common and we can all agree upon is this: we all know when we are personally going through something. We all know how negatively we feel. We all know the many levels of frustration, fear, shame, etc., that we experience during this process.

It doesn't matter what the nature of our "going through" may be, whether it is suffering a loss, being betrayed by someone you love, financial distress, divorce, illness, or anything else. We will begin to demonstrate some kind of physical symptoms once we are faced with these situations for a lengthy period of time.

Some people may not admit they are

> *Any time we don't get what we want, when we want it, we feel we are "going through"*

"going through" when they are. However, there is something about the countenance that often gives us away; our facial features, body language, or attitude may be the culprit. We may even become physically ill.

How we deal with these situations may be more stressful at times than the situations themselves. The manner in which we handle them can have a lasting effect.

This chapter will discuss some of the ways we might respond:

(1) We may try to avoid the issue (I call this the "sticking our head in the sand" response).
(2) Denial or pretending there is no problem.
(3) Blame it on everybody else.
(4) Cry.
(5) Shut down, refuse to discuss.
(6) Harden our hearts (put on a public face).
(7) Victim mentality.

This is not by any means an all-inclusive list, as I'm sure you can think of a few more yourself. Let's take an in-depth look at each of these responses and see what impact they have.

When we try to avoid the issue (sticking your head in the sand), we are not willing to discuss it and just act like everything is ok. We try to continue with business as usual. If someone brings up the subject in our presence, we quickly find an excuse to leave, change the subject, or downright ignore the person. This leaves the issue unresolved, growing, and making things worse because avoidance doesn't work.

When we are in denial, we refuse to accept what has been communicated to us. We may have received news we don't want to hear or believe, maybe even something we never thought we would have to face.

For example, your child is caught with drugs or your spouse is caught with someone else, things you immediately want to refute! My child/spouse wouldn't do that. We view everyone who tries to tell us the truth as the enemy or dishonest. We tell ourselves they are just jealous of us. So, we grow increasingly angry and frustrated because until we accept this is something that has to be faced, things will not get better.

We have all probably tried "the blame game" at one time or another. When this is our posture, we will blame everyone except ourselves: spouse, family members, co-workers, government, religious leaders, and even God. No one is left out as a potential target! Even when we run out of people to blame, rarely do we blame ourselves. We will overeat and then blame it on the food!

This can go on for a long time and become a lifestyle of blaming others for the condition of our lives and why we failed to better. My daddy left me when I was little. My friends turned their backs on me. I couldn't advance because I was blackballed: I was the wrong color, the wrong sex, my hair was wrong, etc. The list goes on as to why we justify our situation. The excuses in the blame game are unending!

Has crying ever been your first response? I know it has been mine many times. Situations that just seem too painful to bear often elicit this response, especially when things seem out of our control. Every time you think about the situation it causes you to want to cry all over again. Honestly, I don't even feel too bad about it; because, when I read stories in the Bible about people like King David and his mighty men crying, I figure I'm in pretty good company!

Crying in and of itself is not a bad thing, as long as we don't live our entire life crying. David and his men didn't! We'll talk more about that later. Crying over the things we can't have on a continual basis is not good. We can take all our cares and burdens to God!

We don't want to let the things we are going through cause us to shut down. Not letting anyone in, internalizing our pain, getting more and more depressed and unable to respond or

> *Even though we may have felt many of the emotions above and wanted to respond that way, we didn't stay there.*

function normally, does not help the situation we are going through. We can't get a different perspective on what is happening if we won't open up.

When we "harden our hearts" we put on a façade to the world. We try to act like it doesn't matter to us. Whatever it is, we can take it. We act as if we are not affected by the difficulties we are facing, that they are of little consequence. We don't want anyone to see our pain, fear, shame, or feelings. Our pride demands we show no weakness. Our shame makes us refuse to let anybody know what is going on. Our world spirals quietly out of control behind the walls we have built around ourselves.

Some of us may take on the "victim mentality." Why me? Something bad is always happening to me! Can't somebody deal with this? I'm too weak! We talk about how bad it is for us all the time. We let every-body know we feel like nobody understands what we're "going through." We feel sorry for ourselves and want others to feel sorry for us. Then they will be motivated to help us out of our difficulties and do things for us we should do for ourselves. We try to elicit others to pick up the slack in our lives so we don't have to get ourselves out of the situation.

Taking charge is when we recognize the situation is painful, yet at the same time realize it has to be faced. **Even though we may have felt many of the emotions above and wanted to respond that way, we didn't stay there!** When we do this, we have some options about how we go through the process of recovery.

We could sit ourselves down, acknowledge the truth and facts involved, and begin to make a list of what needs to be done. We could consult others for their opinions about what they've done in similar circumstances. **But the optimal solution is going to God with the entire issue first!** We can seek His face, cast our cares upon Him, surrender to Him and ask for His direction. Once we take it to God, we must be willing to believe. His Word tells us to "Trust in the Lord with all your heart, and lean not on your own understanding; In all your ways acknowledge Him, and He shall direct your paths" (Proverbs 3:5-6 NKJ).

> *But the optimal solution is going to God with the entire issue first!*

We must be confident of this: He will direct our paths in the midst of it all. Even when we don't know the next step, we must believe. Because we have honestly acknowledged God in the matter, He is going to guide us. He will send us to the right people, open a door previously closed, comfort us in the midnight hour, and encourage us so we know it is well. According to the Bible, God will "…show Himself strong on behalf of those whose heart is loyal to Him." (2 Chronicles 16:9 NKJ).

3

IS "GOING THROUGH" GOD'S WILL?

In John 16:33 (KJV), the words of Jesus tell us, "In the world ye shall have tribulation…" What is the clear implication of this verse? Things that challenge us are going to happen as long as we are on this earth. The word "tribulation" speaks of hard times. The dictionary definition of it is *grievous trouble; severe trial or suffering*.[1] In this particular passage of scripture, Jesus is telling His disciples (including all of us who have accepted Him as our Savior) because we are in this world we are going to go through some rough challenges. However, He tells us to be at peace and of good cheer, because He has overcome the world. He has given us the authority to overcome our challenges and tribulations as well. Hallelujah!

"Going through" is clearly ordained of God, even if you didn't do anything wrong! The Bible says, "Yea, and all that will live godly in Christ Jesus shall suffer persecution" (2 Timothy 3:12 KJV). In exploring what is being said here, we see that Jesus is talking about how He planned for the kingdom of God to function. Let's take a closer look at times in our lives when our "going through" is a result of God's plan.

Persecution means suffering, distress, torment, harassment, torture, teasing, provoking, etc. The situations we discussed in chapter 1 can fit into any of those characteristics or sometimes we may even feel our situation fits all those characteristics. Paul tells us in 2 Corinthians 4:9 (KJV) "We are troubled on every side, yet not distressed; we are perplexed, but not in despair; Persecuted, but not forsaken; cast down, but not destroyed." We recognize that "going through" is not meant to destroy us. It helps shape us. It should not cause us to lose faith or our hope in Christ Jesus. As we see the word unfolding, we see how the happenings in our life are not unknown to God. **He is omniscient, which means He knows everything and nothing is hidden from Him or catches Him by surprise!**

> *He is omniscient, which means He knows everything, and nothing is hidden from Him or catches Him by surprise!*

However, we understand that while going through these challenges, it is all in fact working together for our good. It definitely doesn't feel good at the time, and we sure wish it was somebody else, anybody but us, yet it is still a part of God's plan for us. Jesus himself went through some things, the Bible tells us in 1 Peter 4:1 (KJV) that Jesus suffered for us, so we must be prepared to do likewise: "For as much as Christ hath suffered for us in the flesh, arm yourselves likewise with the same mind: for he that hath suffered in the flesh hath ceased from sin." God wants us to live a life where we do not practice sin! We are called to be a royal priesthood. This is definitely part of the process of sanctification we must go through to become what we are called to be.

His will is for the body of Christ to understand and to expect these events in our lives. These events will cause major challenges for the believer, but also major change! We see this on a daily basis in current times. We believe in the need for prayer in our schools, yet it is currently against the laws of our nation. While there is a move to bring prayer back into the schools, it has not happened as of the writing of this book. There are school shootings, where the very lives of our children are at stake on a daily basis. There is a

His will is for the body of Christ to understand and to expect these events in our lives. These events will cause major challenges for the believer, but also major change.

movement to remove the name of God from our currency. The divorce rate is unbelievably high. Our nation is highly divided. These and many other situations are a reflection of the challenges that will cause conflict in our lives as we strive to live a Godly life! These are some of the external things that will cause us to go through serious warfare.

In the midst of all of this, we must realize God will not leave us nor forsake us and when we inevitably go through these things, we are not alone. We must be aware

> *We know that our challenges are not meant to break us, but oftentimes they help mold us, so we are prepared to live lives that represent Him, that bring glory to His name, and to change us into people who will one day live with Him!*

how we are living out His purpose for our lives. **What He has predestined us for will cause us to go through some challenges.** Some from inside and some from outside. Some things in our control because of choices we've made, and many things not in our control, but definitely all of it within HIS control!

God has allowed some of these things to happen by design, for His plan and purpose for us in the earth to be manifested. The Bible records in John 9:2-3 (NKJ) "And His disciples asked Him, saying, Rabbi, who sinned, this man or his parents, that he was born blind? Jesus answered, neither this man nor his parents sinned, but that the works of God should be revealed in him" and Jesus spits on the ground and makes clay, puts it on the man's eyes, sends him off to wash in the pool of Siloam and he is healed! We don't always understand the why of what God does, and He makes it plain in the Bible that His ways are not our ways and His thoughts are not our thoughts! So, while we do not understand, we can always trust that His plan is to work together for the good of those who love the Lord and those who are called according to His purpose.

Furthermore, the Bible tells us that even Jesus was not exempt from the grievous trouble that befell Him in order to fulfill the plan of God to become the Savior of the world. Isaiah 53:10 (KJV) tells us "Yet it pleased the Lord to bruise Him, He hath put Him to grief: when thou shalt make his soul an offering for sin, he shall see his seed, he shall prolong his days, and the pleasure of the Lord shall prosper in His hand." This tells us God allowed His only begotten Son to "go through" tribulations on our behalf! If He allowed His Son to suffer to fulfill His purpose and destiny, to become our sin offering, and be an example of how we are to live, what about us? We see in multiple scripture passage how those whom He had chosen to "go through" to become were doing what was right in His sight and yet they went through challenges and sufferings. **We know that our challenges are not meant to break us, but oftentimes they help mold us, so we are prepared to live lives that represent Him, that bring glory to His name, and to change us into people who will one day live with Him!**

> *Has it ever occurred to you that God might be doing something in your life when you are "going through,"? Something that may benefit you and somebody else?*

God had a plan for Jesus' suffering. He was to serve as the One who would reconcile us to God Himself, by taking on the sin of the whole world! That we might have a chance to choose Him, to willingly accept His gift of salvation to each of us. This is extremely important in the plan and scheme of what God has in store for us. He wants our challenges in life to make us holy as He is Holy.

Has it ever occurred to you that God might be doing something in your life when you are "going through,"? Something that may benefit you and somebody else? I'm talking about situations that cause you to cry out to the Lord: What am I doing wrong? When will this end? Well, this thought is just what the next chapter is about.

4

GOING THROUGH: GOD-CAUSED VS SELF-CAUSED

Your heart is broken, you're disappointed, it feels like things will never be right again. You feel like you've prayed and prayed and yet God is still silent! You don't know what you could have done to make God angry. The last thing you want is to fall into the hands of an angry God described in Bible. Yet the question burns in your gut — the elephant in the room: What did I do wrong; and if I didn't do anything, then why am I going through so much pain? You read God your resume: "I've been going to church, I pay my tithes, I try to treat people right, I make sacrifices for others, I'm on the usher staff…". Yet you don't see any light at the end of the tunnel, and you're honestly thinking to yourself, "I'm doing my part, God, what about You? Do You even hear me right now?"

When these challenges come into our lives, the above is how we think about what is currently happening. We look at it from how we *feel*. We look at it from an emotional perspective. We react negatively or positively based upon how it makes us feel, whether it is what we want for ourselves or not. Is this what I prayed and asked God for? What could or should God have done to prevent this from happening? Our minds automatically start to dwell on the situation from this viewpoint.

The truth is that there is another viewpoint that we need to consider. It is the most important viewpoint there is: God's viewpoint. How does He see our circumstance? Is He upset about what is going on in our lives, or is He bragging about the type of life we are living?

We discussed the fact that all who live Godly lives are going to suffer persecution. Therefore, we know there is an expectation from God that we will experience some suffering and persecution, which is what we feel when "going through".

Let's review a Bible story that speaks of a Godly man who went through some pretty horrific things, yet he still trusted God. "And the LORD said unto

> *The truth is that there is another viewpoint that we need to consider. It is the most important viewpoint there is: God's viewpoint. How does He see our circumstance?*

Satan, Hast thou considered My servant Job, that

there is none like him in the earth, a perfect and an upright man, one that feareth God, and escheweth evil?" (Job 1:8 KJV). Here God is speaking of a man who loved Him and kept His commandments. Job was truly a man who was about living for God

He wasn't straddling the fence or playing church as some of us do. He was sincere in all of his ways before the Lord. And more importantly, he lived a life that demonstrated his belief. He had a good reputation where he lived. He was a servant to his fellow man. He had the testimony of God that he hated evil. So, we know he did what was good in the sight of God. Even though he was a man of great wealth, we never see him esteeming himself above others because of the money he had. He never failed to help those in need.

With this kind of reputation, this is the last person we would expect to see "going through". Job, however, went through more than anyone else in the Bible, with the exception of Jesus Himself. Think about this: God allowed Job to go through some major calamities. Job, in the span of one day, went from being one of the richest men in the region with ten children, seven thousand sheep, three thousand camels, five hundred yoke of oxen, five hundred donkeys, and a large number of servants; to being extremely poor, where all of his livestock were killed and all his children lost their lives as well! Talk about really going through something! Even his body was afflicted with boils! He endured persecution, suffering, pain, and more. Just in case that wasn't enough, we see later in the story that Job's wife gets involved and advises him to curse God and die. Now his wife wasn't even on his side anymore.

The scripture makes it plain that God allowed Satan to bring this trouble to Job. God also makes it clear that this was not a punishment to Job for anything he had done wrong. We see that indeed God was boasting about how Job was an upright and righteous man. We see Job had not done anything wrong for which he deserved to be punished from God's perspective. What was Job's response to all of the calamities? We see the answer at the end of Job chapter 1 verse 20. "At this, Job got up and tore his robe and shaved his head. Then he fell to the ground in worship". (Job 1:20 NIV) How incredible is that? This man just went through what had to be one of the worst, most painful days ever in recorded history! Not just the death of one child, but ten! All of his wealth gone! Talk about a stock market crash with no savings, no 401k, nothing. Every single investment was wiped out in a single day!

> *No, he does what he has disciplined himself to do: He falls down and worships his God!*

His response to what he had gone through is beyond incredible, to say the least. He didn't do what I would have done or perhaps what some of you might have done. He didn't try to shoot some-body, he doesn't run to the bank and start yelling, "Where is all my money, my land, my livestock?" He doesn't give up and try to kill himself, he doesn't start whining, "Why me." No**, he does what he has disciplined himself to do: He falls down and wor-ships his God!** His attitude in that moment declared God's will was more important than his own. His actions declared he would trust in God who created all things. His words declared he would praise God no matter what! He did all of that with no victory in sight, no hope for tomorrow, and not knowing what would happen next. He didn't have a "word of knowl-edge" that everything was going to be alright. All he had was a right relationship with God that assured him God was indeed in control, faithful, and it all belonged to Him anyway. Therefore, it was God's will to do with as He pleased and Job chose to wor-ship God for everything in the middle of all he was going through! We don't hear of Job ever turning his back on God. We do see he was clearly feeling the agony of all he was going through, because the Bible records how he cursed the day he was born, signifying he would rather not have been born than to live like he was in that moment (Job 3:1). He felt the pain, he experienced the stress of not knowing why these calamities had come upon him, all the time grieving the loss of his 10 children. He was suffering even though he was doing all he knew to serve God.

Job even had so-called "friends" to come and sit with him during his time of grief, which was a customary thing of his day. They were stunned and amazed at the severe and tremendous calamities that had befallen Job. As the time progressed, his friends began to accuse him of wrongdoing. Job took the position he had done no wrong and all of this was in the hands of God. But in the face of so much tragedy, his friends were unable to accept this and declared this had to be something Job himself caused instead of God. His friend Eliphaz says to him, "What man in all the earth can be as pure and righteous as you claim to be" (Job 15:14 TLB) and "How much less someone like you who is corrupt and sinful, drinking in sin as a sponge soaks up water" (Job 15:16 TLB). Job's friend Bildad says to him, "Who are you trying to fool? Speak with some sense if you want us to answer!" (Job 18:2 TLB) and "The truth remains that if you do not prosper, it is because you are wicked" (Job 18:5 TLB) And finally, his friend Zophar says, "I hasten to reply, for I have the answer for you. You have tried to make me feel ashamed of myself for calling you a sinner, but my spirit won't let me stop. Don't you realize that ever since man was first placed upon the earth, the triumph of the wicked has been short-lived, and the joy of the godless but for a moment? Though the godless be proud as the heavens, and walk with his nose in the air, yet he shall perish forever, cast away like his own dung" (Job 20:2-7 TLB).

They brought condemnation down on Job. They added misery to the challenges he was going through. They did not understand the workings of God themselves and could not in their own minds accept this was what God had allowed as opposed to what Job had caused to come upon himself. (Who needs friends like that? They only add to what you are going through.) Job, however, did not waiver because he knew what was in his heart. Even though some of what Job went through may have been brought on because of some personal fear he had: "For the thing which I greatly feared is come upon me, and that which I was afraid of is come unto me" (Job 3:25 KJV). His suffering was definitely not because of sin in his life!

Another example we see in history of "going through" being allowed by God, even when the person is doing His will, is David and his men at the battle of Ziglak. I'm talking about the same David who had an adulterous relationship with Bathsheba, who killed Uriah her husband and other things we could mention. Clearly, David managed to get some things right before the Lord, because the scripture records him as being a man after God's own heart: "And when he had removed him, he raised up unto them David to be their king; to whom also he gave their testimony, and said, I have found David the son of Jesse, a man after mine own heart, which shall fulfil all my will" Acts 13:22 (KJV).

In this particular story David has been on the run from King Saul. He has been anointed to be King over Israel by the prophet Samuel and he finds himself being hunted by King Saul. What had he done to deserve this treatment? Nothing. He had been a faithful shepherd, he had fought Goliath of the Philistines, he had been a talented and skilled musician in the King's court and fought in battles along with King Saul himself. What does he get for his good deeds, things that were in the will of God? Trouble, persecution, suffering and a death target on his back!

All this trouble causes David to run away and make a deal to serve King Achish of the Philistine. This King in turn gives him the land of Ziklag as his own, for him and his men and their families in return for their service. It happens that while David and his men are off fighting, they return home to discover that the Amalekites have burned down Ziglak and have taken captive all of their wives, children and cattle. They are totally devastated when they arrive home. "So David and his men came to the city, and behold, it was burned with fire, and their wives, and their sons and their daughters were taken captives. Then David and the people that were with him, lifted up their voice and wept until they had no more power to weep" (1 Samuel 30:3-4 KJV). After they finished responding just the way I would have, which was to cry their eyes out, they started looking for someone to blame (which is also how I would have responded). They wanted to kill David for the mess they were in. David was in the same mess they were! But they now wanted to stone him.

The thing about David that sets him apart is that he never forgot about who God was, no matter what he was going through. We can't afford to forget who God is either. The enemy of our soul wants us to get so focused on the circumstances that we forget the One who is well able to resolve all our problems. So David encourages himself, he did what he knew to do when he was facing any kind of challenge. He enquires of the Lord as to what he should do. He didn't take matters into his own hands as we so often do. He didn't pick up his gun and say "if I've got to go out, I'm going to take as many of them with me as I can!" No, he went to his source, the God who had been faithful to him in times past. He went to the One he knew he could depend upon. Even though he had done nothing to deserve this situation, he didn't blame anyone. God answers him and restores back unto him and his men all they had lost and more! Think about it: How do we react when we find ourselves "going through" something challenging when we didn't do anything wrong?

In this next example, we have yet an additional instance of God allowing His servant to "go through" when he had not done anything wrong. Possibly a case could be made that Joseph's attitude caused some of what he experienced. Instead, what happens is he begins to trust God for the plan and vision that Joseph had been shown, which we will discuss later. Now, we see Joseph, a young boy with a dream that his brothers were going to bow down to him. His brothers hated him because he was his father's favorite. Joseph didn't make his father show preferential treatment, but like anybody else, he was not going to look a gift horse in the mouth either. In other words, most of us would not turn away extra gifts and neither was Joseph! Joseph ended up in slavery in Egypt when his brothers tried to get rid of him by selling him. Yet the Bible records how God was with him and favored him. "And his master saw that the LORD was with him, and that the LORD made all that he did to prosper in his hand" (Genesis 39:3 KJV).

Even as a slave and prisoner we see how God was with Joseph and he prospered in everything he did, even in those environments that we would definitely call "going through." We never read where Joseph had a pity party. He kept on being consistent. He kept on honoring God with his attitude. No matter how hard it got or how unjust the circumstances were, he would not let any of it cause him to shut down. He modeled what our attitude should be during the storms of our lives.

In the new testament of the Bible, we see other examples of people "going through" when they were clearly doing what was right and pleasing in the sight of God. Paul and Silas were such an example. They were going about spreading the gospel as the Word commands us to do. They went into a city of Thyatira and held prayer meetings. They were followed by a woman with a spirit of divination, calling out after them. Paul grew tired of her doing this, every day. He turned around and commanded the spirit to leave her. "And it came to pass, as we went to prayer, a certain damsel possessed with a spirit of divination met us, which brought her masters much gain by soothsaying: The same followed Paul and us, and cried, saying, these men are the servants of the most high God, which shew unto us the way of salvation. And this did she many days. But Paul, being grieved, turned and said to the spirit, I command thee in the name of Jesus Christ to come out of her. And he came out the same hour" (Acts 16:16-18 KJV).

The next thing they knew they were being hauled before the magistrate, sentenced, beaten, and thrown into prison because the woman could no longer tell fortunes.

What did they do when this unexpected trouble came upon them? The Bible says while they were shackled in the lower part of the prison after they had been beaten, they sang praises unto God! "And at midnight Paul and Silas prayed, and sang praises unto God: and the prisoners heard them" (Acts 16:25 KJV). We see a model of consistency. They demonstrated a relationship where they trusted God with their all. They did what they knew to do. They had a right to have a bitter attitude, and they would have been justified in acting out! However, they did the opposite of what someone would do who had just been beaten up for doing the right thing! They sang praises to God, and so much so that the doors of the prison were unlocked and the jailer himself gave his life to God!

When looking at all of these examples, it's clear how whether it's something God is allowing to happen or part of our decisions that are the cause, God is still with us in the midst of our situations. What this shows us is how a constant acknowledging of God and His faithfulness was the response of those "going through" in God's will. So what about us? What do we do when we are in a negative situation, just because we were trying to help somebody out? Or because we did what we felt God was leading us to do and the results were not what we expected? I can remember a time when my husband was a detention officer and one of the prisoners was going through something and knew my husband was also a pastor and asked him for prayer. When he prayed with the prisoner, he was written up for doing so because it was against the rules. He made the choice to follow

God's leading. Do we follow the examples above, or do we act out of fear and self-pity?

Here is another Bible character that maybe more of us can relate to than we'd like to admit: Saul was the first king God had ever given to the nation of Israel. God had chosen him to be king and only required his obedience and allegiance. Saul did not do as God had instructed him to do when he went to one of the battles he had to fight. He caused himself to be in a lot of trouble with the Lord, and Samuel was the messenger God sent to let him know it!

"And Samuel said, Hath the Lord as great delight in burnt offerings and sacrifices, as in obeying the voice of the Lord? Behold, to obey is better than sacrifice, and to hearken than the fat of rams" (1 Samuel 15:22 KJV). Saul went from being King over all of Israel to being dethroned because of his own disobedience. His excuse was that he feared the people and listened to them instead of God. It is obvious Saul knew what he should have done, but failed to do it. Even when the Prophet Samuel gave him the word of the Lord that the kingdom had been torn from him, he still tried to get God to change his mind. He wanted Samuel to come and worship the Lord with him, so God would pardon his sin. It was too late for that. He had brought a whole lot of trouble on himself that was not God's plan for him. If you study more about King Saul, you will find this was just the beginning of the many troubles he was going to go through because of this initial act. He listened to the wrong people and it cost him everything, even his own life. It really is important to know the people we are listening to, because the wrong people can get us headed down the wrong path in life!

In the New Testament of the Bible, we see an example of a couple bringing on a whole lot of unnecessary trouble to themselves. They caused themselves to go through something they were not able to come out of alive, and all because of their own greed and deceit. Acts 5:1-5, talks about trouble of our own making. This couple, Ananias and Sapphira, planned to lie to the Disciples about a piece of land they had sold to make a donation to the church. The man pretended he was bringing the whole amount the land had sold for, when that was not so. He could have just said he was only donating half, but he did not make that choice. So he died for that choice, to try and deceive God's servants, thereby trying to deceive God Himself. And what makes it worse, he got his wife in on it and she later comes to the temple and tells exactly the same lie and meets with the same punishment. First of all, they didn't have to lie! The land belonged to them and they could have chosen the amount of the land they wanted to give. The choice was theirs. **God always allows us to choose. Jesus died that we might have a right to choose!** At any point in our lives when we are going through different situations, we have the opportunity to choose how we are going to react or act under those conditions. The choices we make will directly affect the outcome. One of the things my husband always says is, "For every action, there is a reaction," and we see this firmly displayed here. We see how the actions of Ananias and Sapphira caused their own deaths.

We also get ourselves in trouble. King Saul did it through his disobedience. Ananias and Sapphira did it through their lying. Most of us have done it through one means or another, whether it was cheating (on a test or income tax) stealing, etc. (You get the idea.) It all boils down to one thing, and that is sin. We can cause ourselves untold amounts of trouble because of our own sin. When what we are going through is because of sin, we have only one way out.

> *God always allows us to choose. Jesus died that we might have a right to choose!*

We need to be like King David and repent quickly. "Against you [God], you only, have I sinned…" (Psalm 51:4 KJV). Although we know God is even quicker to forgive, sin still has consequences and repercussions that we must "go through." Don't think you are not forgiven once you repent, because you are according to 1 John 1:9, which tells us that God is faithful and just to forgive us from all sin and cleanse us from unrighteousness. But this is not an excuse to keep on sinning. The Bible tells us where sin abounds, grace abounds the more! This means there is grace sufficient for us to overcome our own sin.

That being said, there is still a reaction which must come forth. Praise be to God, because His infinite grace and mercy temper these reactions. He said in His word, "He hath not dealt with us after our sins; nor rewarded us according to our iniquities" (Psalm 103:10 KJV). Even though at times we do have to suffer the consequences of our actions, we definitely do not receive all we should when we are "going through". God's mercy is always present, and God Himself has said He will never leave us nor forsake us. This is a true statement regardless of whether we caused what we are going through or whether God allowed us to go through something as we have seen God does indeed do.

5

THE BENEFIT OF GOING THROUGH GOD'S PLAN

Whether we want to believe it or not, **there is a reason for all that we go through in life. It's not all about who caused it or didn't cause it, but about the results it produces in our lives.** The Word tells us that Jesus is going to work on us until the day that he returns (Philippians 1:6). God loves us too much to leave us the way we are. He wants to mold us and shape us into His image. He sent His Son that we might be justified, so it is going to take some transforming on our part (because of the sin nature we are born with) to be what God would have us to be.

> *The problem is that our flesh doesn't want to change. It wants what it wants, when it wants it. We want to do our own thing our own way! Come and go as we please.*

Living a Christ-centered life, the way God purposed us to do on this earth, will take some doing. And it will be a movement of the Holy Spirit in our lives, because we cannot do it on our own. "And do not be conformed to this world, but be transformed by the renewing of your mind, that you may prove what *is* that good and acceptable and perfect will of God" (Romans 12:2 KJV). We must be transformed. The old person we were must die. "Therefore if any man be in Christ, he is a new creature: old things are passed away; behold, all things are become new" (2 Corinthians 5:17KJV). If we do not change we will continue to walk in a way that is contrary to God. And this is not His will for us. We are to follow after His precepts and commands.

The problem is that our flesh doesn't want to change. It wants what it wants, when it wants it. We want to do our own thing our own way! Come and go as we please. God has called us to be greater than what our flesh dictates, and yes we must "go through" to get there. God wants to reestablish

> *When we are obedient, God gets the glory.*

us as in the days of the garden of Eden. He desires His people to have dominion in the earth. He wants to use us to show forth His glory in the earth, because He tells us to let our light so shine, that other men will see our good works and glorify the father who is in heaven (Matthew 5:16). **When we are obedient, God gets the glory!**

Jesus paid a tremendous price to redeem mankind and we are the ones who have directly benefitted from this. God desires all to have a chance to know Him. He wants to use us to tell of His goodness and live lives that reflect His character. That's what the motive of God is all about. He understands for this to occur, we will have to "go through" and suffer. His own Son suffered and was hated and He allowed it to be so. In, fact the Bible says in Isaiah 53:10 (KJV) **"Yet it pleased the Lord to bruise him; he hath put him to grief: when thou shalt make his soul an offering for sin..."** For our part, Mark 13:13 (KJV) says, "And ye shall be hated of all men for my name's sake: but he that shall endure to the end, the same shall be saved." As we go through the things God has ordained for us there are people who will hate us, mock us and say all manner of things about us, just

> *"Yet it pleased the Lord to bruise him; he hath put him to grief: when thou shalt make his soul an offering for sin..."*

as they did about Jesus. It is important that we are not moved by what people say because people will lead us astray.

We will cease from sin if we "go through" properly. 1 Peter 4:1-2 (KJV) says, "Forasmuch then as Christ hath suffered for us in the flesh, arm yourselves likewise with the same mind: for he that hath suffered in the flesh hath ceased from sin; that he no longer should live the rest of his time in the flesh to the lust of men, but to the will of God." Our goal is heaven and we can't make it there on our own. So, Jesus is our example of how to get there, and the way to get there. We must stop what we are doing and start doing what He would have us to do if we are to make it in.

There is a sense of urgency to go through to victory! God is not allowing challenges to be in our way to destroy us, but to bring us to what He has ordained us to be. That we might accomplish what we were predestined to accomplish in the earth and in heaven. "But the day of the Lord will come as a thief in the night, in which the heavens shall pass away with a great noise, and the elements shall melt with fervent heat, the earth also and the works that are therein shall be burned up. Seeing then that all these things shall be dissolved, what manner of persons ought ye to be in all holy conversation and godliness…" (2 Peter 3:10-11 KJV).

The benefit of heaven is a great incentive. However, heaven is not all He has for you. God has rewards for His people who keep His commands. The Bible tells us that eyes have not seen nor ears heard of the things that God has prepared for those who keep His Word (1 Corinthians 2:9-10). He also gives us opportunities to do great and mighty things in the earth as His representatives. "Verily, verily, I say unto you, He that believeth on me, the works that I do shall he do also; and greater works than these shall he do; because I go unto my Father" (John 14:12 KJV). We have the opportunity to spread the gospel as never before, by far greater means than were available in Jesus' day.

We have redemption and justification as His benefits, health and provision are all a part of His salvation package. Just having the honor of being in right relationship with God. Being called His Beloved Children is truly benefit enough! Being allowed to be His representatives in the earth is an added bonus! "Now then we are ambassadors for Christ, as though God did beseech you by us: we pray you in Christ's stead, be ye reconciled to God" (2 Corinthians 5:20 KJV). We are called to declare His Glory, no matter what situation we are going through at any given moment. This is an opportunity afforded to only those who belong to Him. Even when we are challenged, we must still give praise and honor to God. He wants us to model ourselves after Him even when we are "going through". Luke 6:35-36 (NKJ) puts it this way: "But love your enemies, do good, and lend, hoping for nothing in return; and your reward will be great, and you will be sons of the Most High. For He is kind to the unthankful and evil. Therefore be merciful, just as your Father also is merciful".

"GOING THROUGH" IN A MANNER PLEASING TO GOD

Knowing there are things in our life that are going to be difficult, yet still ordained for us, should give us a sense of relief. Knowing we are not being punished for something we did wrong, we should be able to glorify God in the midst of the storms in our lives. It pleases God when we do this. "In everything give thanks: for this is the will of God in Christ Jesus concerning you" (1 Thessalonians 5:18 KJV). This doesn't mean we give thanks for every bad thing that happens. It means we give God thanks in every circumstance, good or bad.

Going through in a way that pleases God will mean self-sacrifice. There is no way of getting around it. Our flesh is going to have to die if we are to please God. We are not going to be able to weather the storms of life in a God-pleasing manner without dying to ourselves. What does dying to ourselves really mean? It means focusing on God instead of our-selves. When we find ourselves in a specific situation, if we become more concerned about God being glorified in the midst of it than fearing the outcome, that is when we become more God-conscious. We are no longer saying, "What is going to happen to me? Am I going to get what I want? Will it go in my favor?" **When we are at the point where we can say with total honesty and mean it from our hearts, "Not my will, but thine be done Lord," then we are in a place to "go through" in a manner that pleases God!**

Some of us may say, "How can God really expect such a thing of mankind? After all, we're only human." And you're absolutely right. However, He does expect exactly that! He said in His Word we are to give thanks in whatever situation we find ourselves because this is His will for us. What? That we give thanks for our tragedies? Thank Him for the death of a loved one? Thank Him for the loss of my house? Thank Him that my husband of 25 years just walked out on me? No, I reiterate, He is not saying thank Him for the tragedy, but thank Him in the midst of the tragedy. Recognize that He is the only one who can resolve it! There is nothing you or anyone else can do about it! There is

> *When we are at the point where we can say with total honesty and mean it from our hearts, "Not my will, but thine be done Lord," then we are in a place to "go through" in a manner that pleases God!*

no point focusing on ourselves and not acknowledging the One who is well able to help us overcome! He is able to comfort us when nobody else can "And I will pray the Father, and he shall give you another Comforter, that he may abide with you forever" (John 14:16).

God is willing to meet every need. When the banker has stamped foreclosed on the books, we have to say, "But my God shall supply all of your need according to his riches in glory by Christ Jesus" (Philippians 4:19 KJV). He tells us He will exceed our request: "Now to Him who is able to do exceedingly abundantly above all that we ask or think, according to the power that works in us" (Ephesians 3:20 NKJ).

Why? Simply because He loves us. He does what He does because He loves us! He doesn't leave us as we are because He loves us too much to see us living in a manner that will not lead to our good and His glory. He makes it plain in His word how He wants the best for us, "for I know the plans I have for you, says the Lord. They are plans for good and not for evil, to give you a future and a hope" (Jeremiah 29:11 TLB). God has good plans for us! He has high expectations for us and doesn't want any of us to miss heaven and the rewards He has in store for us! "The Lord is not slack concerning his promises, as some men count slackness; but is long-suffering to us-ward, not willing that any should perish, but that all should come to repentance" (2 Peter 3:9 KJV). He wants to bring us to a place of victory in every situation. "Now thanks be unto God, which always causeth us to triumph in Christ…" (2 Corinthians 2:14). It is the loving will of a Father toward His children, to see us living the abundant life. The Bible tells us He came that we would have life and life more abundantly (John 10:10).

This is still His love for us. It is His expectation for His people. He didn't send His only begotten son to die for us, only to watch us get tangled in earthly temporal situations and miss His best for us. It isn't His desire to see us living beneath what He ordained for us as His children. He does not desire to see us struggling against circumstances and situations one after another. He desires us to rejoice and give thanks. "My brethren, count it all joy when ye fall into divers temptations" (James 1:2 KJV). His love for us is greater than all of these things! Knowing of His love is reason enough to give Him thanks in the midst of our storm. Knowing the Word says "There hath no temptation taken you but such as is common to man: but God is faithful, who will not suffer you to be tempted above that ye are able; but will with the temptation also make a way to escape, that ye may be able to bear it" (1 Corinthians 10:13 KJV). He has given us everything we need to be successful. "According as his divine power hath given unto us all things that pertain unto life and godliness, through the knowledge of him that hath called us to glory and virtue" (2 Peter 1:3 KJV).

We must find our "Job's praise" as I call it. Job fell down and worshipped the Lord in the midst of the greatest storm of his life. He focused totally on the Lord, he didn't focus on the calamities that had befallen him. Had he done so he would never have fallen down and worshipped God. He may have fallen down and starting crying and beating his fists on the ground. Had he done so, his thoughts would have been wrapped up in himself, what he had lost, what he didn't have anymore, and how he would ever survive. Why did the Lord do this to me? We of our natural selves wouldn't blame him! But God has a different expectation for us, His people. He has shed His love abroad in our hearts and He has greater expectations for us than we know. He has and will put enough compassion in us if we will seek Him and not focus on the situation.

His grace is sufficient for every situation. The only way we are going to walk in God's expectation, is to believe on His Word! "But without faith it is impossible to please him: for he that cometh to God must believe that he is, and that he is a rewarder of them that diligently seek him" (Hebrews 11:6 KJV).

As we lovingly turn our focus to Him in the midst of our challenges, we must believe that He wants the best for us! "Every good gift and every perfect gift is from above, and cometh down from the Father of lights, with whom is no variableness, neither shadow of turning" (James 1:17 KJV). He desires to give us the best, and God doesn't withhold any good thing from those who are in right standing with Him. It is going to take faith in Him to receive those gifts. We see this in the scriptures as Peter began to walk on the water in Matthew 14:29 (KJV): "And he said, Come. And when Peter was come down out of the ship, he walked on the water, to go to Jesus." Once he had gotten over his fear, Peter was able to step out and walk on the water just as he could see his Master doing. As long as his focus was on Jesus, he walked on water. The mercy of it all is that when he began to sink he had enough sense to call out to Jesus and Jesus reached out and saved him. The storms in our lives are like that as well, and God is willing to save us.

As long as we keep our eyes on Jesus we are well able to overcome with praise, peace, and joy. When we take our eyes off Jesus and focus on our troubles we begin to sink into doubt, depression, despondency, disappointment, and self-pity. This is not the way God wants us to be. He wants us to live lives full of victory, with the attitude that speaks what the Bible says: "I can do all things through Christ which strengtheneth me" (Philippians 4:13 KJV). This should be our motto. Therefore, giving thanks unto God in the midst of our storm is not too hard. We are well able to do it through Christ (trusting in Him, because He loves us). "Jesus said unto him, If, thou canst believe, all things are possible to him that believeth" (Mark 9:23 KJV). Choose faith, make the choice to believe God's Word. Choose to live wholly committed to the Lord and you will give Him thanks in everything, as this is His will for us and He, the God of all living, will be pleased with you.

THE GARDEN OF VICTORY
OR DEFEAT?

What does it take to go through the challenges of life in such a way that honors God? What does it mean to have joy in the midst of a storm? Is it even possible? Honestly? How do we "go through" without fussing, or cussing, or acting unseemly, or being totally disagreeable?

So many times when we are "going through" it can be easily seen on our countenance. Our lips are stuck out, pouting! Our attitude is bad! We don't want to talk to anyone! If we do talk, we are short and abrupt with others! Some of us choose to put on a façade and act as if nothing is wrong. We pretend all is good. We use our church lingo, "Yes, I'm too blessed to be stressed," but any discerning person can see the sadness, confusion, and fear in us. Yes, I did say fear because that is one of the main things that causes us to "go through". We are afraid of what may or may not happen, we're angry because we are not in control and it all began in the Garden of Eden. It leads us to question whether there is anything we can do about this state of being.

How do we overcome these very natural tendencies? The tendencies that come from being in the image of man instead of God. "And Adam lived a hundred and thirty years, and begat a son in his own likeness, after his image; and called his name Seth" (Genesis 5:3 KJV). Once sin occurred, we became aware that we were inadequate and experienced what it was like to lack. Before the sin of man in the garden, we were not "going through" because there was no perceived lack. Everything we needed or desired was there for us! Let's look at this concept in-depth, because herein lies the secret of going through to victory.

Adam and Eve were in right relationship with God in the beginning. I would proclaim to you that the victory was in the relationship. As long as they fellowshipped with God, they were walking with Him in the cool of the day. They were keeping His commandments. In other words, they were following His instructions. It was completely well with their souls. They didn't lack anything. They didn't need anything. They had no complaints. They lived in the most beautiful place there was. Perfect temperature, perfect surroundings in every aspect. Not too much of this or too little of that. Indeed, paradise on earth. No rude, obnoxious neighbors, no mean bosses, just peace and tranquility. Not a care in the world. That was the nature of their relationship with God. I believe this is still the nature of the relationship God wants to have with us today. **Our relationship with God determines the level of victory in our lives!**

As we have examined in the scriptures, we see the level of victory and relationship correlation conclusively demonstrated again and again in the lives of the men and women of God who had a right relationship with Him. We won't confuse perfectionism with victory. Nor is being perfect a precondition for victorious living in Christ because truly everyone has sinned and fallen short of the glory of God according to Romans 3:23. We have all gone astray, "And changed the glory of the uncorruptible God into an image made like to corruptible man…"(Romans 1:23). We have tried to replace the spiritual things of God, with the intellectual things of man.

We should know by now that God will do the very thing we are least expecting. He has made it plain we can't possibly think like He does (Isaiah 55:8-9). The twists and turns in our lives are designed to make us more Christ-like, to shape us into those holy vessels He is coming back for. He is the potter and

> *Our relationship with God determines the level of victory in our lives!*

we are the clay. Gods plan is that we be conformed

into His image. "For we are his workmanship, created in Christ Jesus unto good works, which God hath before ordained that we should walk in them" (Ephesians 2:10). God is calling us His workmanship. He continues to work on us daily. He will do so until the day Jesus returns. He uses the circumstances in our lives to bring us back into relationship with Him.

God uses yet another garden to do the necessary work for us to become what He has created us to be. Jesus, in the Garden of Gethsemane, set the tone and example for us to come to God. He established victory over the flesh and succored our salvation even before the actual act of the cross, by His submission to the will of God.

God leads us to empty and broken places so we have nothing to lean upon but Him! We transitioned from the way of living in the Garden of Eden to the state we are in today. It is a state where we are lost without intervention from a loving and merciful God, who wants us to live in the victory He purchased for us with His shed blood. The enemy of mankind thought he had defeated Jesus when He went to the cross; therefore, he thought we were defeated as well. Satan did not know it would truly be a victory for Jesus, signed,

> *God leads us to empty and broken places so we have nothing to lean upon but Him!*

sealed and delivered, or he would have created a

different game plan. But since God is ultimately in control, and it is His plan that is in effect in the earth (even though it looked from the outside like Jesus was caught and there was no hope) the truth was, that victory was already won for eternity!

IT IS NECESSARY

*I*n concluding this book, let me share with you one final perspective on "going through". Maybe you've noticed it as an overriding theme, but if not, allow me to point it out to you. **I would ask you to consider the perspective that it is necessary to go through to become what God has ordained you to be**. Because success from God's perspective *is* becoming what He created you to be. Therefore, this process of "going through" is extremely important! The Bible says Jesus learned obedience by the things He suffered. In other words, the things He went through are the very things that caused Him to be who He was and to accomplish what He did. He had to fulfill His destiny. To become the savior of the whole world, He had to go through something. Isiah 53:5 says He was wounded for our transgressions, bruised for our iniquity, and by His stripes we are healed. The very sin we deliberately do, the lies we've told, the gossip, the people we've mistreated, the pride and arrogance we've exhibited, every sin of ours caused Jesus to "go through"! The Bible further records He was marred beyond recognition. Do you think it would have been painful to go through all of that, and all for someone else?

Jesus suffered (went through) the things He did so we could choose salvation. This is what was prophesied about Him – that He would go through these things, that He would suffer many things. If the King of Kings and the Lord of Lords had to suffer many things in fulfillment of His purpose, shouldn't we expect to do likewise?

When He was at His lowest point He didn't look around at His circumstances for someone to blame. He was found in the garden of Gethsemane looking heavenward and talking with the Father. He didn't desire to go through what He was about to go through, but He was willing to trust God with what He had to do. It was totally His choice to obey God. We see Jesus in a posture of surrender and trust, fully committed to the plan and will of God.

The struggle was real and it is evident in the fact that Jesus cries out in the garden "And he went a little further, and fell on his face, and prayed, saying, O my Father if it be possible, let this cup pass from me; nevertheless, not as I will, but as thou wilt" (Matthew 26:39 KJV). It was clear Jesus was in great agony, more than anything any of us will ever experience! So much so that the Bible records how His sweat was like great drops of blood! (That is some serious going through.) Can you imagine knowing the weight of every sin and sickness that ever exist was about to be laid upon you? And in that very moment those closest to you would abandon you, pretend not to even know you? **Jesus went through all He went through *for us!***

So, what should we be doing? Why shouldn't we go through things to fulfill our destiny? To be successful in what God has ordained us to be. Jesus always modeled what we are to live like in this earth. He's our example of how to live *in* this world but not *of* it. Our job is to follow the example He left for us. We are to look to Him for our help, because all of our help comes from the Lord. Down through history there were those who knew the secret: Jesus was teaching us through His lifestyle.

The Apostle Paul new the secret! According to Acts 9:16 (KJV): "For I will shew him how great things he must suffer for my name's sake." God had told the Prophet Ananias in this scripture that He would show Paul, who was then Saul, what things he must suffer for the gos-

> *Jesus went through all He went through for us!*

pel's sake, and He did. Yet the Apostle Paul is credited with writing two thirds of the New Testament! Some of it was written while he was "going through", locked up in prison. This is how he describes what he went through in the Bible: "Thrice was I beaten with rods, once was I stoned, thrice I suffered shipwreck, a night and a day I have been in the deep" (2 Corinthians 11:25 KJV). Acts 28:3 (KJV) says, "And when Paul had gathered a bundle of sticks, and laid them on the fire, there came a viper out of the heat, and fastened on his hand." We see where he was expected to surely die from a venomous snake bite. But in spite of all he went through, he didn't let it stop him from doing what God called him to do. The Bible records how Paul was told by the Prophet Agabus in Acts 20:23 (KJV), "Save that the Holy Ghost witnesseth in every city, saying that bonds and afflictions abide me," meaning he would be bound and afflicted if he went to Jerusalem and he still went knowing what was to happen to him. All these things happened to Paul once he had given his life to Christ. Because he went through, he was able to become what God ordained him to be and accomplish great things for the Kingdom of God. "Now God worked unusual miracles by the hands of Paul, so that even handkerchiefs or aprons were brought from his body to the sick, and the diseases left them and the evil spirits went out of them" (Acts 19:11-12 NKJ) These things were accomplished because he was an anointed vessel, called of God, intimately acquainted with Christ's sufferings. All of this happened while being in an intimate relationship with God (just like they were in the garden days), walking humbly and completely submitted to Him.

Even in Paul's submission to God and the things he endured, he went through things God did not change or release him from. 2 Corinthians 12:7-9 (NKJ) reads like this: "And lest I should be exalted above measure by the abundance of the revelations, a thorn in the flesh was given to me, a messenger of Satan to buffet me, lest I be exalted above measure. Concerning this thing I *pleaded* with the Lord three times that it might depart from me. And He said to me, 'My grace is sufficient for you, for My strength is made perfect in weakness.'" This passage

> *Sometimes we don't get the answer we are seeking from God.*

is widely debated as to what exactly Paul's thorn was. Some say it was sickness, an eye issue, or perhaps as some kind of disturbance during his meetings. Whatever the case, he begged God to remove it three times. God's response was no. He was told to live with it by God's grace! He tells Paul that in his weakness, God's strength is sufficient. That goes for us as well. **Sometimes we don't get the answer we are seeking from God.** The loved one who was faithful dies, a divorce happens, financial devastation occurs! But note how God says His strength is available in these times! We just have to choose to lean on Him and depend upon Him instead of relying upon our own understanding. We have to recognize there are going to be hard places we have to live through to become the anointed vessels God has predestined us to be. At that point we can choose to trust Him and celebrate that in our weakness/challenges God is still there working out His good plan for us. Or we can rebel against God in despair. It's our choice: Worship and praise our way through, or cry and moan our way through!

Historically, we see many other great figures in the Bible going through to become what God had ordained them to become. Some of these we've mentioned in earlier chapters. God makes no distinctions between people, which means we too shall go through some sufferings on the journey to becoming what God wants us to be. For example, we see Joseph, the favorite son with his brand-new coat of many colors, oldest child of the mother, beloved by his father. He didn't have to work out in the fields as did his brothers. God showed him dreams and visions of how all his family would one day bow down to him. Sweet life, right? But he was hated by his brothers! He was hated so much that the brothers couldn't stand to be in the same room with him. At their first opportunity, they sold him into slavery, and lied to their father saying he was killed by wild animals!

Having been sold into slavery by his brothers, Joseph had to go through some major challenges. He went from being his father's pampered and beloved favorite son to being a slave and a prisoner. He went through, even when he was doing the right thing! However, the things Joseph went through changed him into the man he needed to become to fulfill his purpose and destiny. The dreams and visions Joseph had as a young boy were indeed dreams of his purpose. He was not at that time ready to be the man of those dreams. He went through life's challenges: loneliness, loss, abandonment, mistreatment, unjust persecution, and being forgotten. All of this he went through to become what God had ordained for his life. I imagine to myself that if Joseph had become second in command over all of Egypt before he had gone through the challenges of life, he would have had a very different response the next time he saw his brothers! Because all he had been through, he was able to say he would not punish his brothers for what they had done to him. The Bible says, "But as for you, you meant evil against me; but God meant it for good, in order to bring it about as it is this day, to save many people alive" (Genesis 50:12 NKJ). He was mature enough and had gone through enough to see the bigger picture, not just a picture of himself.

Another example we see about the need to go through to become is David, the King of Israel, anointed by the Prophet Samuel. After David was anointed to become King, he went right back to the field to tend his father's sheep. It would be nearly fifteen years before he actually became King. He went through many challenges in the years between his father's fields and the throne of Israel. He killed Goliath, the giant warrior of the Philistine nation. He had to run for his life, hide in caves and scrounge for food when King Saul sought to kill him. King Saul was relentless in his pursuit of David. Saul's jealousy over David's fame in battle, and the knowledge that the Kingdom had been taken away from him because of his own disobedience, made him hate David. It made him determined to make sure he would not be his successor! On at least two occasions, David could have killed Saul; but because God was molding him to be a man after His own heart, David did not do it.

What is the protocol of God toward us going through some things? We know God has said in His Word He is a God who changes not. I believe this means He has not changed how He deals with His people. So there will be some things we are ordained to go through to become what God has in store for us. What is going to make all the difference is our attitude while we are going through it. In the three examples we looked at in this chapter, we see a commonality resulting from their going through to become what God had ordained for them. They walked humbly before God and were totally submitted and committed to God. Both traits are foundational for doing great things for God. We must never try to make a name for ourselves at the expense of using God's name, or the gifts that He has bestowed upon us. This is the attitude Jesus and these great men exhibited. We must also exhibit these attitudes if we are going to do the greater works we are to perform. These mentioned were successful at becoming what God had called them to be and at fulfilling their purpose.

Now is the opportunity to trust God in the midst of our situations. Right now all kinds of challenges are going on in our economy, churches, government, sickness, pestilence, panic and pandemonium all over the world. Now, is the time to cast all our cares upon Him because He cares for us. Now is the time for us to totally surrender all. We must realize that nothing happening in our lives or that will ever happen in our lives is unknown, too difficult, or too challenging for God. He knows all and sees all, and it is His desire that no one should perish. He doesn't want us living stress-filled lives of fear. He wants us to thrive and to have abundance. Once we are in right relationship with Him, having accepted Jesus Christ as our Lord and Savior, living a consistently obedient lifestyle, then we are ready to fulfill our destiny and become what He has ordained us to be. Will we be perfect? Absolutely not! However, we should be in pursuit of the perfection of a loving God who has great things in store for us! "Beloved, now we are children of God; and it has not yet been revealed what we shall be, but we know that when He is revealed, we shall be like Him, for we shall see Him as He is" (1 John 3:2 KJV).

Let's enter into God's rest so we can live the abundant life he has ordained for each and every one of us. I'd rather face anything I have to face knowing God is on my side. What about you? We each get to choose. So why not? Go ahead, go for it! Stir up the gift within you! Increase your faith by hearing the Word of God! Go through with confidence that God is going through with you, to bring you into what He has planned for you. Knowing that you are not alone and that God is refining you for His good purpose, should allow you to have peace in the middle of life's storms. Therefore, you are able to go through with a Godly attitude that declares God's favor upon you no matter what, **because what you ultimately become is on the other side of through!**

What you ultimately become is on the other side of through!

ENDNOTES

1   Dictionary.com, s.v. "tribulation," accessed December 17, 2019, https://www.dictionary.com/browse/tribulation.